THE HANDBOOK TO YOU

Discover How You are Programmed and How to Live Your Life to the Fullest

MICHAEL SESSIONS

JONES MEDIA
PUBLISHING

DEDICATION

Amanda, Lilliana, Kam, and Mila—you are my life. I love you!

CONTENTS

AUTHOR'S PREFACE

Great spouses are there to support and encourage you to be the best you can be. My wife is no different. I have been running a company for over twenty years, and my wife knows my business as good as anyone, and she told me one day, "You have a lot of knowledge you could share with people; you should do a podcast." I said, "That's a good idea. And what exactly is a podcast?" She laughed and explained to me what it was, because she had had some experience with a small business she was running. And I thought, *What a great idea for the people that work with me to have a library of information on a podcast.* And anyone who knows me will tell you I really love to talk, so I started a podcast called the *Sessions Effect*. You can find it on iTunes, Google Play Music, and Stitcher Radio.

The *Sessions Effect* has been very successful—we have over 300,000 downloads on iTunes alone—and contains twenty years of my entrepreneurial experience along with studies I've done. It's been a blast doing, but the best part is it has helped a lot of people. And that's exactly why I did the podcast. I want to help people live out the life they've always wanted to live and be amazing, and if I can share something with you that will help you change your life for the better, that is why I get up every day.

After success with the podcast, my wife again encouraged me, "You should write a book and put all your ideas from the podcast in the book." Now, the podcast was one thing because I have a gift to talk, but writing a book? I was the worst English student ever, not a great speller, and the only thing that saved me in school was being good in math. So, the idea of writing a book was a bit scary, but things you learn in this book will help you get out of your comfort zone and assist with learning why you are programmed the way you are. We are either creating or disintegrating. I must get out of my comfort zone just like everyone else if I want to grow. I liked the idea and let it sit for a bit.

A couple weeks later, I was talking to a business partner, Cory Capone, and he reiterated the same idea. We were finishing up a call one day and he said, "Hey, Michael, by the way, you know your podcast is pretty good, you should take all those ideas and put them together in a book." Ok, so that is the second time in two weeks someone has told me to write a book. I just laughed to myself. *Ok, I guess I should write a book.* (And I would have to say, "Thank you, Cory, for reiterating what my wife told me, to write a book.) So, here we are.

How could I not write a book when my purpose in life is to help people live the life they've always wanted to live? I love seeing people win, especially when they don't think they deserve it, feel they're not worthy enough, or simply just don't know how to win. This book was written so people can finally understand why they are the way they are and how to achieve anything in life they want. I will teach you how to get anything in life you want—and no, it's not all about money, but I'll teach you how to get that too. At the end of this book you will feel more confident in yourself, have a plan on how to win, and understand how to improve your results and live a life of fulfillment. And, the best part is you'll have the information to share and help someone else. The world needs more love and compassion and people sharing amazing things with each other.

Sit back, relax, and enjoy the ride as you learn about some amazing things I hope will help transform your life for the better with this instruction booklet I put together consisting of twenty years of experience. I know this material has changed my life.

ACKNOWLEDGMENTS

I would like to thank God for all the amazing blessings in my life, the person you made me, and in advance for all the amazing blessings to come.

A very special thank you to my mentor and coach, Bob Proctor, who has given his life to helping people grow with his information and study. To all my family, personal friends, and mentors who have always been there for me no matter what. You know who you are. I love you and I am grateful for you. Also, to you, the reader, for being brave and courageous and taking that leap of faith to work on yourself and being the best you can be! Let's have fun.

INTRODUCTION

Have you ever been seeking something new or longing for better results in your life? Are you looking for a massive change in your life?

Feel stuck or maybe depressed, going through the motions day to day?

Motivated but don't have direction?

I WAS all of these!

There I was, sitting on my couch in my brand new custom-made home. My wife and I had been designing this house for five years, mostly in our minds, and then eventually we built the house. I had been running my company at that point for 16 years and had achieved a lot of success. I am happily married with three amazing children and a dog. My kids were going to the schools we wanted them to go to, we were driving the cars we wanted to, we had the house we wanted, great friends, and we had our health. Life was amazing.

On paper, many people would have wanted my life. So, why did I feel stuck? I'm fulfilled and happy, my life is amazing, so the question for me was: *Is this the pinnacle?* Had I reached everything in my life I could from a business perspective?

I am 41, life is great, and I have zero things to complain about, so was this the top, or was there something more? More than that, I wanted to put a finger on what made me successful. How did I get here besides running a good company? What did I do to make myself successful? Was this the top? So, I went searching…

I started watching every motivational video of Tony Robbins and Bob Proctor I could. I was reading books on Earl Nightingale and Napoleon Hill. I quickly realized the success I had up to this point wasn't because I was necessarily skilled in so many areas, but more so the way I thought about the things in my life up to this point. I had always learned from a young age that if you have a great attitude you were probably going to do well. Now, there were times in my life when things weren't so great, but I always found the positive in the situations. I always told myself, *If you want success and to do well, you need to have a great attitude. If you do, then you will find success.* But was attitude the only thing? I knew a ton of people that had amazing attitudes, so could attitude be the only thing?

As I started studying and learning, I realized there's more to success and happiness than just having a great attitude. You can control the results in your life. You can literally attain any goal you want to reach. It wasn't by doing certain things, but by doing things a certain way. Could thinking a certain way really be that powerful? If so, then anyone could do it, and that excited me. As they say, when the student is ready, the teacher will appear. And I was ready to find the answers.

I started learning ways people can change their life by doing very simple things. I also learned why I was programmed the way I was. I sought out validation for why I had been so successful, and it wasn't just skill—there was way more to it than that. I finally got the explanations on how I had gotten to where I was, and now, how I was going to move forward from this point. I studied with mentors, read books, and listened to audiobooks for over four years. The puzzle was coming together on how I had gotten to this point in my life. Every day I couldn't wait to get up and learn more.

Once I started learning, all I wanted to do was share the information I was learning, because what I was learning was information anyone in the world could learn and implement.

My purpose in life and my "why" has always been to help people live the life they have always wanted and become whatever they want to become. Also, educating people on the fact they don't have to just "get by in life" has been a driving force for me. You can thrive and achieve and be what you dream of being. Like myself. I just needed the coaching and knowledge.

There are handbooks to everything in the world, from how to fix your car to cooking to raising children to traveling the world... The list goes on and on. But there's never been a handbook for YOU. A book that describes who you are, how you became who you are, and how to ultimately teach you how to be everything you want to be—until now!

The Handbook to You will help you step out of your comfort zone and understand the negative habits slowing you down, teach you how to form habits that will change your life forever, help you set <u>real</u> goals that will get you out of bed every morning with a passion, and ultimately help you have a positive impact on your family, your work, and the world. You will leave the world better than when you found it, and that is amazing.

The contents in this book come from twenty years of studying, personal development, and experience which have changed my life and blessed me with the tools to help change your life. I know someone will change their life forever after reading this book. The material in this book changed my life, and I can teach you how to change your life, too.

1

THE MASSIVE POWER OF YOUR THINKING

"Thoughts can produce tangible things from the
formless substance."

Wallace Wattles

This chapter could be one of the most important things you'll ever read in your life. It is one of the reasons I wake up every day. My wife and children are reason one, but I'm very passionate about this idea.

Everything in existence was started with a thought. Look around and pick something up. I'm going to do it with you. I'm picking up a highlighter. It's laying on my desk. This highlighter started with someone's thought. Someone said, "Hey, why don't we make something that can highlight things and we can put it into a pen form?" And now we are holding in our hands a highlighter.

Your thoughts can produce physical things. Let that sink in for a second. You can produce physical things with your thoughts. For example, Thomas Edison, Wright Brothers, Mark Zuckerberg—all their inventions began with a thought. All had ideas in their mind that were repeated over and over, eventually becoming a physical thing.

Your thinking mind is that powerful. What I want you to understand is how to use it to your advantage, not against yourself.

Let's talk about attitude. Teachers, counselors, your boss, your coach will explain that if your attitude improves your grades will go up, your marriage will be better, you will improve at your job, and you will play better. This is something that is very important to us all. However, if you ask twenty different people what attitude is, you will more than likely get twenty different answers. Attitude is what we need to alter to get the results we want, which means it is very important. Something this important we need to get clarification on. When someone says you need to have a great attitude, this is what attitude is. It is not simply cheering up, there is more to it. Attitude is made up of three components: thoughts, feelings, and actions. It is not just your thoughts and feelings, but when your thoughts and feelings are combined and expressed in your actions. We get to internalize our thoughts and draw conclusions on those thoughts, which determines our feelings and actions.

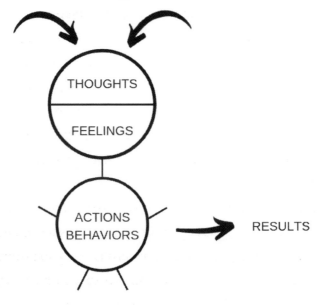

We live in a thought world. How you think determines your life. Science and theology are really the only place we can go for proof of things. They have both agreed on a common point, which is we get what we think about over and over. So, if these two industries can agree on that, then thinking must be important. I believe it's our most important responsibility, and the great news is I can teach you how use it in your favor.

How do you know you are thinking the way you need to? By looking at the results you're getting in life. Your results are a direct reflection of how you are thinking. If your results are not good, then you must change the way you're thinking. If your results are excellent, then you are thinking the way you need to think. Everyone has the ability to think. The man on the street corner has the ability to think. The doctor who checks you out once a year has the ability to think. Everyone has the ability to think, and it's one the highest functions you are capable of. Thinking is the most potent form of energy there is. If you want to know how you or someone else is thinking, just listen to what they talk about. If people were thinking, they would not say half of the things they say. Have you ever thought of what you think about in a day? Take a minute and write down the top ten things you think about and check off the things that improve your life. I know, a little scary, right? I felt the same way.

So, then, if everyone has the ability to think, why don't they? Mainly because they are not aware of how important the way they think is to their life.

It's not easy to think the way you need to. We have been programmed to think by our heredity, genetics, and environment. We live in a world of negativity. The news has everyone scared. That's their job. The news is to make you scared so you keep watching. I don't watch the news. There's nothing good on the news, and most of it is not true. They program you with fear, and if that is how you are thinking, then the result is fear. You walk around looking for the solution on the next news hour and hope for better news. It never happens. The local baseball team lost again. It's going to rain. It's going to be hot. Someone got shot... It goes on and on. Don't clog your mind with negativity. It's difficult to think positive when the appearance is negative. You might be saying, "Well, Michael, my situation's kind of crummy. I'm in debt. I don't like my job. You're telling me to think positive?"

Yes, I am. If you don't change the way you think, then you will stay in those situations.

I'm telling you to think positive. Change the way you think, change your results. It's not easy, it's going to be one of the harder things you do, but it is vitally important. People that live in poverty will continue to live in poverty unless they change the way they think and what they think about.

We have to train our mind to think the way we want to think. No one can make you think anything you don't want to think.

For example, if you do sales for a living, the appearance might be you're not very good at sales, but the reality is you're amazing, you're intelligent, you're powerful, and you're confident and good. Thought is that powerful. Don't let what's going on in your life keep you from thinking the way you need to. Don't let the appearance of what is going on in your life determine the reality. Once again, that is not easy, I understand, but if the Wright Brothers can think us into flight, then you can think your way out of debt or whatever challenges arise in your life. We are not going to talk about how to fix your thinking right now, though, that will be in a later chapter. All I want you to do right now is understand the concept. Thinking is the most potent form of energy there is, and what you think about determines your results in your life.

Let's now discuss what happens when a thought comes into your mind. There are many parts to your mind, obviously, but for what we are discussing we are going to focus on two areas: conscious mind and subconscious mind.

Let's start with your conscious mind.

In your conscious mind you can accept or reject any thought. If you don't like a thought, you can kick it out, and likewise, if you like a thought you can accept that thought. Most of our thoughts were programmed to us by our parents. That is why you like the sports teams you like and the foods you like, for example—because your parents like those things and taught you to like them too.

You can choose where you collect information. The conscious mind is where we gather knowledge. We go to college, we study for the test, we pass the test, we get a grade, and if the grade is good enough we get the degree. It's where your sensory factors are stored, where you see, hear, smell, taste, touch. *Hey, that smells good. It's lasagna. I like lasagna, so when I smell lasagna I have a positive thought.* You can accept or reject any thought you want in your conscious mind. Most people go their entire life only using the five senses to make decisions on things.

SEE, HEAR, SMELL, TASTE, TOUCH

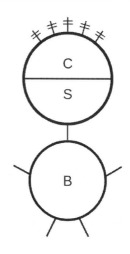

In your conscious mind, when a thought is accepted over and over it moves to your subconscious mind. It's impressed upon your subconscious mind, and that's where feelings come from. The early Greeks talked about heart, and that's what they meant. Through repetition in the conscious mind, thoughts are stored in the subconscious mind.

This is where your feelings come from.

I'll give you an example. The first crush you had, you accepted a thought you really liked that person. From that point on you thought about the person over and over. The more repetition you gave to the thought, it was accepted by your conscious mind and then turned over to your subconscious mind. That is when a feeling is produced, and then you move into action. Your body starts acting according to the feeling you tell it to have. Suddenly, you are doing things you didn't used to do because of the feeling. The feeling of that crush moved you into a positive energy, which produced positive results. Remember when your parents said to do your chores, and because you had a feeling of love you said, "Ok, no problem, I will do my chores" without a second thought? It is because of how good you were feeling.

Your results are based on those feelings produced from an action that returned good results. Even if the result was not perfect, due to how you were feeling it didn't faze you.

I have friends that watch the news a lot. They've accepted from the news that we live in an unsafe world, and whatever the news says is true. They have accepted a thought, produced a feeling from it, and the action is worry. Opposite of the example above. They basically walk around worried. Not a good way to live. Who wants to walk around worried? In fact, I think we live in a very safe world, but the news would make you think we live in a very unsafe world where right around the corner is danger. Did you know a lot of people in the Great Depression became wealthy? Not everyone was standing around a trashcan with gloves with no fingers warming their hands by a fire. There were many millionaires made in the Great Depression because not everyone accepted the thought they were in a depression. Not everyone accepted the thought that life was crummy. A lot of people did. "Hey, it's a Great Depression, so we're just going to go with it, go with the flow." You must protect your thoughts.

Your conscious mind is not developed until you're about six years old, so all you have in your early years is your subconscious mind. Your subconscious mind is wide open for learning. That's why if you've ever met a four-year-old that can speak three languages it blows your mind. Children are learning sports, different languages, how to play different instruments, because their subconscious is taking it all in.

Your subconscious mind does not have the ability to reject any thought. Your subconscious is totally deductive, meaning it only accepts what you tell it to accept. It's like the earth, for example. If you plant corn in the earth then corn will grow. If a foot over from that corn you plant deadly night shade, a poisonous plant, the earth will grow that also. So, consider your subconscious as the earth, in that whatever you give it to grow, it will grow. If you're telling it to grow thoughts of fear, anxiety, and nervousness, then you're going to create those feelings, which will produce actions and results that will not benefit you. Likewise, if you are telling it happy and healthy thoughts, it will produce those. Those thoughts will produce actions and results you want.

You were taught to think by your heredity, environment, and family. Everything your parents gave you went directly into the subconscious and started growing there. Once again, this is the reason kids learn so well. As they are young they are taking everything in— good and bad, unfortunately. All of these thoughts over and over create habits, and these habits are saved in the subconscious mind forever—unless they are replaced with a new habit to take their place. You don't have to think the way you were taught to think. But most of us do, including me. Good news is we can change the way we think. Your thinking is your highest responsibility. No one else can make you think anything you don't want to think.

It's not easy to change the way you think, though. I'm not here to tell you it is. I'm here to tell you, you can do it, you can change the way you think, and you can start living the life that you want to live, and you can start being successful and getting the results you want. Dream about it. Think about it over and over. Reject the negative. You have the ability to reject the negative. Stop and consider what you think about in your day to day life. If science and theology have agreed we get what we think about, then we must stop and consider what we are thinking about in our day to day life. If you're not getting the results in your life, it's based on your limited belief of what you're telling yourself. Get excited about something you want. What do you want? Most people feel they don't know what they want, but I think they do know what they want. They just need to explore the thought that they can have anything they want. I will teach you how to get whatever you want in a later chapter. For now, understand your thinking determines your life and results.

I love talking to and having an impact on people.

For now, once again, just focus on what you think about. Have you ever taken a step back and really processed what you think about daily? It's a pretty interesting thing. If you listen to certain people, it's obvious they do not try to process what they're thinking about. This is no judgment to anyone, but you can tell by the way certain people speak and the negativity that comes out that they're not thinking; they're living a life that's been programmed. You have the ability to think what you want to think. Now, whatever you decide to think, positive or negative, starts to build a little house in your subconscious mind and gets stored there over and over, and then your subconscious mind produces feelings based on those thoughts, good or bad. A person can have whatever he or she wants. I've given you the examples of the Wright Brothers, bicycle mechanics who had an obsession of flying. There are numerous other people that did the same thing, in that they figured it out—like Sir Edmund Hillary, the first man to climb Mount Everest. It took him three times, but he never lost the thought and the obsession he could do it, and sure enough, the third time he got to the top of Mount Everest. He was a beekeeper. In recent times, Alex Honnold has become the only person to ever climb El Capitan, a 3000-foot granite rock, without a safety rope. Might seem a little scary to most, but serves as a great example of how we can think into existence the results we want. Every touch of that climb could have meant death, but Alex was able push past that for the result he wanted. I love this example of how powerful our minds are. Further, if he can do that then we can for sure think better results into our lives.

It doesn't matter what industry you're in. Start to think. Put those thoughts in your mind. You get the choice. And let me be specific here: the results you're getting and the life you have are a direct reflection of the way you think. There are no exceptions to this rule. You get what you think about, and you get the choice to think in your conscious mind and form habits in your subconscious mind and feelings, and that causes the actions and behaviors which provide the results. That is how results happen.

" The results that you are achieving are a direct reflection of your image of yourself... change your image, change your result "

2

YOUR TWO IMAGES

Have you ever wondered how you became you? Why you act and think the way you do? It isn't just random luck. You were programmed that way, by your environment and heredity.

In 1960, Dr. Maxwell Malts published a book, *Psycho Cybernetics*. Psycho cybernetics is an interesting term: psycho is Greek for mind, cybernetics is science of control and communication. You have a control mechanism in your mind, and it's going to determine what comes into your life and how well you do. We refer to this as an image, or a self-image.

Dr. Maxwell Malts, a plastic surgeon, made an amazing discovery in 1960. When working with his patients to fix a deformity or scar and wanting to increase the appearance of his patients after surgery, he noticed a significant increase in their appearance along with a significant increase in their psychological state and how they felt about themselves. He also discovered no matter how perfect the surgery went, and in some cases, even though the appearance had improved, the patient saw no increase in psychological stimulation or effect. In other words, they felt the same even though their appearance had improved.

Dr. Malts concluded we have an outer image as well as an inner image. The surgery would improve the person's outer image, but not always the inner image.

Our outer image is how we present ourselves—the way we dress, do our hair, makeup, our appearance. Our inner image is how we view ourselves and what we think of ourselves, and if you have a negative or a bad image of yourself your results are going to be a direct reflection of that image.

Our images have been programmed from our environment—friends, family, neighborhoods, heredity, etc. A child that's raised with praise grows up to be a confident adult, and a child that's raised with criticism grows up to be a very insecure adult. Now, confident people understand the dynamic of who they are and the power of their mind, and they like themselves and have a good opinion or good image of themselves. Those who don't understand themselves and are super critical of themselves and feel inferior have a poor image. Either way, you can improve upon your image and the way you view yourself.

We have an enormous number of higher creative faculties, such as reason, will, intuition, perception, and imagination to name a few. But they get burdened by false concepts and doubts, and it's our responsibility to get rid of these false concepts and doubts so we can feel amazing about the person we are.

So, how do we do this? How do we create the image we want? Well, first, it's important you understand you, and the more you do, the better image you're going to have of yourself. Your image operates like a missile shot from a plane. The missile will bounce off course multiple times until it hits the target, with cybernetics being the device that keeps it on course. We operate in the same manner if our inner image is the same. No matter how many times we try to change it we will go back to that inner image. Thus, the importance of making sure your inner image is one of beauty, love, and confidence.

Again, this is all based on self-image. Let's just say you have a self-image that you are a little heavy. You want to lose some weight and you work hard and lose ten pounds. But if your inner image of yourself is that you're heavy, cybernetics is going to deviate back on course and you're going to go and find that weight again. And it will bring it right back to you.

Your self-image determines everything. It determines your confidence level and how you interact around and with certain people and situations. How do you change your image if you are not happy with the one you have? Well, first you must understand you have an image of yourself in your subconscious mind, and life operates by images.

Your results are a reflection of your image. And if you don't like your image, the good news is you can change it by consciously and purposely choosing the kind of person you want to be. We can sit down with our amazing mind and start thinking, *What and who do I really want to be like?* And then you pick the people you really like and start to emulate that person. You're not copying the person, just the qualities you like.

When we were little we had a hero or a character we always pretended to be. We walked and talked like this character. We pretended to have the image of that person, and our inner image of that person became ours until we grew out of it.

Now, as adults we need to sit down and write out a description in the present tense of the person or image we want to have. Writing out the description of the person is an attempt to improve your self-image. Start to see yourself as that person. This is called imagined reality. This is an actor's technique, so if you're an actor you know what I'm talking about and what this means. Before they take on a role, actors will read the script to see if they can fit as that character. Once an actor accepts the role, he or she rereads the script, memorizes it, internalizes it, and then becomes the character he or she is playing. That's what you want to do. Most people are extras in their own movie, but we don't want to be an extra in our own movie. This is your life. This is your movie. You want to be the star in your movie, so you want to learn how to act the way you want to act and have a positive image of yourself. Write your own script. The image that's fixed in your subconscious mind is how the rest of the world is going to see you. No one can alter your two images but you. No one can do it for you, but you sure can do it. So, begin living the life you really want to live. See yourself as everything you want to be: happy, healthy, wealthy, confident, effective. Really love yourself. When you wake up in the morning, hug yourself. Give yourself a big hug and say, "I love myself. I love you." Give yourself a big kiss every morning. Build a great image of yourself, because what's on the inside will be reflected on the outside, as we've talked about before. The wisest scientists can't begin to guess what you're capable of.

Remember from *Psycho Cybernetics*, whatever your self-image is, when you deviate from that image the cybernetic mechanism in your subconscious is going to take you right back to that image. If you have a great image, you feel great about yourself, you love yourself, but even when you get down you get off track. That cybernetic mechanism is going to bring you right back to that confident self you are. And remember, the results in your life are a direct reflection of the image you have of yourself. When you improve the image, the improvement will automatically be reflected in your results.

So, here's some questions for you. If you want to work on your self-image, how would you describe your self-image? Is it a true image of how you feel about yourself? Or are there differences between what you project and how you really feel about yourself? Do you have a positive self-image? Is there room for improvement? Now, I think there's room for improvement for anyone, and I've fixed my self-image over the years. I had different self-images throughout my life. When I was in college, I was broke, in debt, and I didn't have a great image of myself. No one likes feeling broke or being in debt, so I let the outer image of my life create the inner image. That inner image was not a true reflection of the special person I was. Unfortunately, until I started to believe I was awesome, effective, and on my way to success, I was going to stay right where I was.

I changed the way I looked at myself. The appearance was I was broke and in debt, but the reality was I was a successful entrepreneur. I jotted down the people I wanted to emulate to achieve the way I wanted to live and the person I wanted to be. What would you like to improve about your self-image, and is there a person you can think of you admire and respect? Think about their qualities. Write out a description in the present tense of the qualities you admire about that person. Once again, we're not copying the person, everyone is their own unique, amazing self, but focus on the qualities of the person you would like to emulate in yourself.

You don't have to believe the image you feel about yourself. If it's not good, just remember, you can be awesome. You can be everything you want to be. It's going take some work, but it can be done. You create the image you want, and you live in that image of the person you want to be. I want you to be amazing, and I love that you are putting in the effort to better your life by reading this book.

Also can do this exercise for your team.

25

That makes me happy, because if you're self-improving and you're working on yourself, you are a hero, because someone is going to be impacted by you someday because you took the initiative to improve your life. The result of that is someone's life will be changed for the better because of you. You will have the confidence someday to give it to someone else. That could change their life forever. All because you had the courage to work on yourself. That is awesome.

These first two chapters are just laying the groundwork on your thinking and what you think about and how your thinking is the most important responsibility you have. Secondly, how you view yourself and your outer and inner image. In later chapters, I am going to teach you how to fix negative thinking and negative images. For now, I just want you to understand where and why we think certain things about ourselves. When I first understood these first two points I had a sense of hope I could start change for the better, and I got so excited. My hope is you are too. Let's keep growing.

If your external world is a mirror image of your internal self image what is it telling you about how you see yourself?

How would you describe your self image?

Is there a difference between my projected image and how you really feel about yourself?

Is your self image a limiting paradigm or is it strong & empowering? What does that inner dialogue look like?

What are the Qualities you love about yourself? & How do we bring those Qualities out more?

3

WHY WE DON'T PERFORM

There's a big gap in what we know and what we execute. School teaches us when we're growing up to read the book, listen to the professor or the teacher, take notes, study for the test, get a grade, and if you get grades consistently enough that are decent, then you can get a degree or you can move to the next grade.

So, we've been taught from a young age to absorb knowledge, gain knowledge, and in fact that's how we've rated people on whether they're intelligent or not. The ability to gain knowledge and then regurgitate it on a test has become important, and the more knowledge we absorb is supposed to mean we're supposed to be producers or to be smart from a company standpoint. Companies in North America spend $70 billion a year getting their employees trained to know more information. However, they fail to train on how to execute. They train on getting information. Getting knowledge in school doesn't teach us how to execute. School never taught me how to make decisions. It also never taught me how to make money. Now, I gathered knowledge in school, but knowing something and executing and doing it is a huge gap with, I would say, almost everyone, including myself. We can always do more.

We know enough, but why don't we perform? You look at effective people in companies across the country, and they execute, get the job done. What are they doing someone else is not? They use the same presentation, the same closing techniques, they have the same material, the same information, so why do they get a different result versus someone else in the company with the exact same knowledge?

It lies in the paradigms. A paradigm is a multitude of habits, an idea that is fixed in a person's subconscious mind that causes them to do something without any conscious thought. Further paradigms control your subconscious mind, which moves you into action and controls your results. We have talked about your subconscious mind in Chapter One. For example, I'm breathing right now. I don't have to tell myself, "Okay, Michael, time to breathe." No, I'm just breathing. It's an unconscious habit I developed in the womb.

Now, there's good and bad paradigms. The person who's getting the job done and getting effective results has changed the negative paradigms in his or her life and developed a new habit of the successful skills, and they use that to get the desired results. Or they have been raised in an environment that has programed them confidently as a person. Let me give you some examples of good paradigms: confidence, giving, preparation, safety, peace, serenity, belief, positive creator, trust, calmness, responding. These are all good habits, and if we program these habits into our mind daily, we're going to get a better result. Remember, a paradigm is nothing but a group of habits stored in your subconscious mind.

Here are some examples of negative paradigms that slow us down: insecurity, greed, procrastination, fear, worry, doubt, negativity, competitive, skepticism, anger, guilt. These are all examples of paradigms that slow us down.

So, how can one know if the paradigms are good or not? Look at the results you're getting in life. If your results are not what you want, you must go to the paradigm. It's the difference between knowing something and doing. You know what to do, but why are you not doing it? It's the paradigms.

Let's review our mind from Chapter One for a second.

The conscious mind is connected to the world around us through our senses. We can hear, see, smell, taste, and touch, and we've been raised to live through our senses to gather information, positive or negative, so we accept or reject the thought. In your conscious mind you have that ability, and we make evaluations based on our conscious mind.

The subconscious mind is the part of the mind that expresses whatever is impressed upon it. Let me repeat that. The subconscious mind is the part of the mind that expresses whatever is impressed upon it. The expression is what we refer to as doing. Your subconscious mind is where your feelings are created, which determine whether you're effective or not. We have genetic programming from our conscious mind, our subconscious mind, and we have environmental programming.

Genetic programming, for example, with DNA, is the reason we look like our parents. We've been genetically programmed to look like them, and typically we act like them. Environmental programming is way more important than genetics. If you were a baby born in the United States and your parents took you to China and decided, "Hey, we're going to live in China," you would grow up learning Chinese and have no knowledge of the English language unless your parents decided to teach you English as well. You grow up programmed to learn Chinese, so you're being programmed by your environment.

Become aware of your actions that are habitual and nonproductive.

What are some actions you have that are habitual and nonproductive? These non-productive activities slow us down and keep us from getting the results we want. I want to give you an example of a paradigm and really what it could do to your effectiveness. Think of a school bus. The engine on a school bus has a governor on the engine. It keeps the engine from going past fifty miles an hour for safety reasons. There are children on the bus, there's no reason for a bus to be going fast. However, the engine has more horsepower. It can go eighty miles an hour or faster, but it's governed to go fifty. So, these negative paradigms are the habits we have which slow us down, or put a governor on your ability and potential—and we don't want to do that. We want to take that governor off. We want to throw that governor away and unleash potential and not be held back anymore.

Come up with some nonproductive habits you have. Habits that don't benefit you in your daily life you wish you could change. Once you become aware of these habits, you can likely see a common error. The error is you have habits that are not productive, and you are trying to get results that are productive. This is not the approach we want. Once I see people becoming aware of this they try to change by changing behavior, and when this happens the change is generally temporary, because when behavior changes typically you get a good result, or you get a different result. That result gets you excited. But don't be fooled, because behavior is not the primary cause, it's a secondary cause. The primary cause is the paradigm, and we're going to get into how to fix the paradigms in the next chapter. Once again, I just want you to become aware of the paradigms at this point.

So, common error is trying to change the paradigm/habit by changing the behavior. It's good you change behavior if you want to get a different result, but that's a secondary cause. The primary cause is that deep-rooted habit in your subconscious mind you're mostly not aware you even do. We must fix that if we want to fix our results. Write down some nonproductive habits you notice in your weekly and daily routines, and go back and write down some productive things you do in your daily and weekly routines. Let's start to identify the productive and nonproductive habits we have.

As you start to become aware of these paradigms, these habits that stir us up, you're going to have the keys to the kingdom. You're going to be able to go and do the things you've always wanted to do, and you're going to start living the life you're supposed to.

Most of us are confronted with the same challenge every day. We're doing things we don't want to do. We're getting results we don't want to get, and for some strange reason we continue to do these things anyway. Over and over again. Why does this happen?

We see people frustrated. They're not getting results they want. We also see people who are highly educated not getting the results they want. Educated and non-educated not getting the results they want. When you know something and you know how to do it backward and forward, up and down, and you've done it before, why then, all of a sudden, do people stop doing what they already know how to do? You look at a professional baseball player, for example. You'll hear about a player getting into a slump and he can't seem to hit the ball anymore or can't seem to field the ball and throw it over to first base. It's as if he never played baseball before.

Once again, they know everything there is to know about the game of baseball. They've hit the ball 10,000 to 20,000 times. Now, suddenly, it's as if they never played the game before. The non-productive paradigm steps in and controls behavior. This paradigm will keep showing up periodically until the new positive paradigm is made. The frequency of it showing up is determined on situation. So, if your daily life requires you to perform, then we have to understand these paradigms.

People don't even know that this is what's slowing them down. That's the scary thing. It's like a toxic gas you can't smell or see. Paradigms are nothing but a multitude of habits logged into our subconscious mind, and our subconscious is what puts us into action and causes the behaviors we have, which gives us the results we do or don't want.

You can get the results you want in your life. Whatever you want, you can get. It's a matter of understanding the things that slow us down. Why would I not do something I know how to do or have done before? It's the paradigms. Now, step one is understanding what a paradigm is and that it's creating your results. Step two is if you know paradigms control you and you're still letting them keep you from getting the results you want, then we're going to try to work on that and help you with changing the way you talk and think about yourself on a daily basis. So, get excited. You will make progress and start to improve.

Take our example from earlier in the book on kids who speak multiple languages because all they do is absorb. That's why when you're little you get involved in different instruments, sports, and hobbies: because you're absorbing, and these habits form life experiences. We want habits to form life in a positive, not negative way, so if you're not getting the results you want in life, it all goes back to the paradigm, the habits you have.

It doesn't matter whether you know something or not. Look at the results. Results come from behavior, and behavior is caused by a paradigm, and the results tell an interesting story: the story of how the person is programmed.

We can no longer let the negative habits slow us down. Let's take the negative habits that get in the way of us doing what we already know how to do and getting the result we should be getting and change them. Every time a negative habit arises we're going to do the opposite. If you're tired or not growing in your company, then quit focusing on not growing. Focus on being the next best leader in your company. As we start to understand these paradigms and these habits we've been programmed with from a small age, we can start to get ahold of why we're not doing what we want to do and what we already know how to do.

The paradigms will not go away unless you work day in and out to change them. I don't care what your paradigm is, if you want to change, it will require work. I can show you how to change the paradigms which are keeping you from getting the results you want.

Remember, behaviors produce actions, and these actions are ultimately how we get results. When you focus on the paradigm helping you to understand why you're doing what you're doing, everything will start to change. It's not bad luck. It's not where you're from. It's not your situation. It's the habits. What you believe about your situation is a habit, and the good news is habits are formed through repetition, so they can be changed. I can show you how to do that utilizing the tips and ideas in this book.

The next chapter is where everything changes.

"When you get, give and when you learn, teach."
Maya Angelou

4

How to Change Paradigms

This chapter has the ability to be a game changer for you. It will literally give you the instructions to control your life and allow you to do the things you have always wanted to do. As we just discussed in Chapter Three, paradigms control our behavior, and that behavior controls our results. Therefore, if we want to change the results, we have to change the paradigm. *Warning: If you just change the behavior then the change will be temporary. Behavior is a secondary cause. The primary cause is the paradigm.*

So, how do we change the paradigms? Remember, a paradigm is nothing but a group of habits stored in your subconscious mind, and these habits control our behavior and results. Once again, we have good and bad paradigms/habits. Most of the time we're not even aware of these habits. And these habits are the ones today we're going to start to change. Are you ready to change your results and your life? Let's go.

What I need you to do is get out a piece of paper, and on that piece of paper I want you to write down a negative result you wish you could change. This could be personal or business related. Below that result you are not happy with, I want you to write out all the non-productive activities associated with that negative result. For example, let's say you are unhappy when it comes to your income. What you would do is write down your income as it is currently, and let's just say your current income is $60,000 a year, and you don't like that and wish it was not the result and you want it to be higher. Let's say you do sales for a living. You would want to write down all the nonproductive activities associated with that result of $60,0000 you are not happy with. Let me just add that you are grateful to make $60,000 a year, however, you want that result to increase. Negative in this case would be a result you want to change. Once again, we have the result we don't want and the non-productive activities associated with the result.

Here is how it would look on the paper: *I am not happy making $60,000 a year and want it to increase. My sales go up and down monthly, I am not consistent with my sales. I get insecure when the month is coming to an end and I have not reached my goal for the month. Customers trust me sometimes, and other times I don't know that they're listening to or trust me.*

Now, we have this all down on a piece of paper, including negative results you don't want along with all the non-productive activities that are associated with that result. Take a second and look at the negative thoughts you have written down that are associated with that result. You can visually see in the sentence the negative paradigms. Those are the paradigms we want to change.

Now, I want you to take that piece of paper in a safe place and burn it, shred it, or tear it up. It's symbolic. By doing this you're not going to change the paradigm, but what we're trying to do is symbolize the old paradigm leaving and going away, and now we want to establish the new paradigm we're going to train into our minds and follow.

In other words, we are going to create a new model we want to live by. Grab another piece of paper and write down the result as you would like to see it going forward. Maybe you want your income to be $120,000. Write it down on the piece of paper. Then you want to write down the paradigms that are opposite from those on the first piece of paper you burned. Here is an example of what you would write down to improve your result and to change the paradigm: *I am so happy and grateful now that my income is $120,000 yearly, my sales are consistent, I am confident in myself and with my results, customers trust me and enjoy my time, and I surpass my goal every month, and I love it.*

As you can see, these are the exact opposite of the negative paradigms from what we first wrote down. This is the Law of Polarity, which states everything has an opposite: up and down, good and bad. Therefore, if we can be bad at something, we can be good at it. We will be discussing all laws to building wealth and fulfillment in later chapters, but for now I wanted to introduce you to this one law. If we can be inconsistent, then we can be consistent. Now, there are a couple of rules with what we are doing. Remember, we are reprograming the new habit to replace the old, nonproductive habit.

Rule One: We have to start our new idea with gratitude and in the present tense, which is why we say, "I am so happy and grateful now that…" If you are not grateful for what you have you will not attract anything more. It doesn't matter if you have nothing. If you can breathe then you have life, so you have something. Further, we want to live in the present, as if we are already the things we wrote down. For example, "I am so happy and grateful now that my sales are consistent daily, customers trust me, and I am effective every day, and I love it." Not in the future, not in the past, right here and right now.

Rule Two: You have to say your new idea out loud, as there are vibrations in your voice and those vibrations determine what you attract.

Rule Three: You must have faith in what you are reading. If you just read it and don't believe things will change, the exercise is pointless.

Rule Four: You must concentrate when you read it.

Rule Five: You must repeat it as many times in a day as you can. I want you to take a minute and read out loud what you wrote three times in a row. I know you are smiling. If you are smiling after reading it three times, then imagine what will happen if you do this every day for the rest of your life. You will live the life you have always wanted. The behavior is going to change because you like the new way you are feeling, but a warning, behavior is temporary and a secondary cause. The paradigm is what we have to change. What we are doing is creating a new model we want to live by. Another warning: as we learned in Chapter Two, about our images, if you don't work on the new habit long enough for it to be permanent, then cybernetics will bring back the old image you had of yourself, and that is not what we want. Make a commitment right now that you are going to work on yourself for the rest of your life. We are only going in one of two directions: ahead or backward. We are creating or disintegrating. There is no other direction.

Now, we want to work on three paradigms at a time. Get those down and work on three more. If you work on too many it becomes counterproductive. We are auto-suggesting, or self-suggesting, to our subconscious mind the result we want.

I say to myself every day, "I am so happy and grateful now that I am happy, healthy, and wealthy, and I love it." As I say this I feel amazing and continue to focus on happiness, health, and wealth, not sick, broke, and sad.

Many people tell themselves this, but they don't have to. Now you know you can train a new habit for life that you want to see.

We are programming a new habit using that amazing mind of ours to create the new habit, and after a while the new habit is established, and that's the habit you start to live. Now, you might think this is a silly exercise, but if you study it and do it long enough, you'll realize it's not silly and is effective, because that's exactly how you were programmed with the negative paradigms, through the repetition of the negative habit. The only problem is you were too little to be aware of the programing. Your environment programmed it for you. If you look at the good things you do in your life, those were programmed as well. *I'm so happy and grateful. My income is $120,000. My sales are getting better every day, my results are continually going up, customers come to me on a daily basis, and I hit my bonuses on a weekly and monthly basis, and I love it.* You write the script. Remember, it's your movie.

Write it, say it, repeat it as many times in a day as you can until that habit is programmed into your results. I want to give you a personal example of how I changed a paradigm. When I was in seventh grade my parents woke me up to go to school and my mom and dad had alerted me there had been a situation and there was a lot of police and a SWAT team in our neighborhood. I grew up in small town in Virginia, and I lived on a mountain. What happened is two convicts escaped a prison, stole a car, and the car had run out of gas at the bottom of the mountain we lived on.

The convicts got out of the car and hiked up the mountain, and the line they were hiking, there were two houses in between my house and where they started. The first house they got to was locked. They then tried to break into our other neighbor's house and couldn't, but the owner had left his keys in his van, so they stole the van. They ended up crashing the van into a tree pulling out of the driveway, and then went to the next house. At that house, unfortunately, there was a double homicide. There were two children, who were fine, they had crawled into a crawlspace under the house. As I rode on the school bus down the mountain that day there were police cars everywhere, along with SWAT teams holding semi-automatic weapons. It literally looked like a scene from a movie.

As I learned about the story throughout the day it was obviously very disturbing to me. As my family got home we didn't know if the initial convicts were the only two that had escaped. There was still a lot of tension surrounding our neighborhood that day. I remember coming home that night and our neighbor walking into our house with a gun by his side and going in and making sure our house was clear and none of the other criminals that could have escaped were hiding in our house. And I remember that moment sitting in the car watching this happen. It was a very traumatic thing for me. Now, this is when I was in seventh grade, and as time goes on I remember that story from time to time, and it never really bothered me until I had children, and then just the thoughts over the years of that story had been programmed into my subconscious mind.

I didn't even know that this fear from so long ago was still luring inside until I started having children. A few years into having children, I vividly remember waking up one night feeling overwhelmed with anxiety and fear. My fear was I wouldn't be able to protect my family in time if someone broke into our home. My paradigm was fear, and it was literally keeping me up at night. Paradigms are that powerful.

The fear was a paradigm that was deeply planted in my subconscious mind many years ago, not surfacing until later on in my life. I didn't understand how powerful the fear was that I had planted in my subconscious. It was a paradigm, but I didn't know it at the time. A wise mentor of mine was consoling me one afternoon about my fears and anxiety. This meeting was one I will never forget. My mentor asked me, "What would you tell your son if he came running into your room and said, 'Daddy, Daddy, the bad guys are here, what should we do?'" And I said, "Well, I would tell Kam, 'Buddy, it's okay. Daddy's here. We live in a very safe neighborhood. We have a guard, our doors are locked, and we have an alarm.'" When I was not the one in harm's way it was easy to see the answer, but I still had to convince myself of that. Once again, the opposite of fear: safety.

My mentor suggested I get a picture of myself when I was a little boy and have that same conversation with the little boy in the picture. I found a picture of me when I was a kindergartener, and every day I would say to that picture, "It's okay, buddy, we live in a safe neighborhood. The doors are locked, we have a guard at the front gate, we have the alarm on and everything's going to be okay." It literally took me a couple months to reprogram that fear away from myself because I was scared. I would wake up and hear something and was really in a place of fear, but if I can be afraid, then I can be safe. Law of Polarity says I can have the opposite of what I feel, and that's an example of a paradigm, a serious paradigm that is no longer a part of my behavior or life on a daily basis. I don't worry about anything like that happening anymore, but did you see how I had to take the new result I wanted and physically tell myself as a young child that it's okay?

It is important to remember, if you plant negative seeds every day and you harvest those negative seeds, you're going to get the negative results, and you're basically giving oxygen to all the negative paradigms. We talked about how to change your life, to live the life you want. You can do it. Anyone can. You just have to believe enough in this process. Paradigms are nothing but a group of habits, a multitude of habits, and habits come from repetition.

Since you can't change other people, then the blame is inappropriate. Blaming others causes a person to remain in the same spot they've been in, a prison of their own making, and when you take responsibility blame is eliminated and you are free to grow, and those that don't take responsibility for their lives and their results find themselves in this mental prison, and in many ways this mental prison is a much worse place to live than an actual prison. Mental torment can destroy just about everything that is necessary for a meaningful life. You are responsible for all the results in your life. Let me just repeat that. You are responsible for all the results in your life, good or bad. You are responsible for your happiness, your health, your wealth, your emotional state, regardless of what has happened in the past. The future lies ahead with an open slate waiting for you to take control and create a wonderful life for yourself and those around you. I want to leave you with a quote from Winston Churchill, who certainly knows something about responsibility. "Responsibility is the price of greatness." Promise me you'll go back and study this over and over until you understand how to change the paradigm. Once you fix a couple of the paradigms, like I did, then you work on a few more until you're getting the results in your life you want. This is not something you can change overnight, it will take time and consistency. If I can overcome my paradigms, then you can, too. I happen to believe we're God's highest form of creation and he wants us to be amazing and to live out our fullest potential. Don't get slowed by these habits that were programmed into your subconscious mind. As you start to change paradigms your behaviors will change right away just because you're excited about this, but you have to stick with it. You can't do this for a week and say, "I'm good, I have changed the paradigm." All you have initially done is changed the behavior, and it feels good, but remember, behavior is the secondary cause. Keep going, because you have to change the paradigm, not the behavior. It won't be easy, but you have to push forward. You can do it. I believe in you, so you should believe in you.

5

CHANGE YOUR MIND:
THE GENIE.

You know when you look around at successful people in any area and ask those people, "Hey, what did you do to be so successful?" Have you ever really noticed they don't actually say anything? I mean, they do say things, but it's never anything where you go, "Oh, if I do that then I'm going to go be successful." For example, take a sports game when it is over. There's going to be an interview with one of the players, and I want you to listen to what those players say.

The reporter will ask, "How did you overcome adversity and bring your team to victory?" The player will answer with something like, "Well, we stuck together as a team. We executed our game plan and we made the shots when we had to, and that's how we won." Now, that is what they did, but that's not really what they did. Some of you might be scratching your head right now, but I'm going to explain it to you. Next to how to change the paradigms, this chapter is most important. This is going to give the answers on why you've been successful in your life or why you haven't, and is really going to be a game changer for you.

Tell me what color your car is. Does it have two doors or four? You now have a picture of your car on the screen in your mind. Now, I want you to tell me what your front door at your apartment or house looks like, and I want you to be aware of the picture of your front door that just came on the screen in your mind, and now I want you to think of a red balloon. Now there's a picture of a red balloon on the screen of your mind. Now, I want you to think of your mind. What's your mind look like? If you're like most people, an image of the brain appeared on the screen of your mind, but your brain's not your mind any more than your elbow or your kneecap. Once again, we think in pictures. The problem is no one has ever or will ever see the mind. But your mind is what we have to change if we want to live the life we want to live. Your mind is in every part of your body. The mind is not a thing. It's an activity. Your mind is an activity, and it is either in a confused or orderly state. Doctor Thurman Fleet created an image to bring order to the mind. Since we think in pictures, having a picture helps bring us to a calm state. Here is a picture to help.

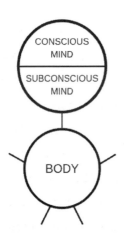

Now, the brain is a part of your body, and it's a magnificent part of your body, but your brain is actually an electronic switching station. The image brings order to the mind. Whenever we begin to think of the mind, confusion sets in because no one's ever seen the mind. Confusion causes feelings we don't appreciate. Dr Thurman Fleet created this image, and it is called the genie. You get to decide your thoughts, which determine your feelings, and then produce results. The reason it is called the genie is, like a genie, your mind will give you what you ask for. Now we have a picture we can use to help us have clarity of the picture of our mind.

The top level we're going to label your conscious mind, and the bottom level your subconscious mind, and the little circle below we're going to label your body, and we want to operate from a premise that we're on three levels: mind, spirit, and body. Those are the three levels that we're dealing with when it comes to ourselves as people and how we function in the world. Your conscious mind is the thinking mind, and most people use their conscious mind to make decisions on things.

That's where we get to decide what goes on. It's where we gather knowledge. Most people use their senses to determine how they think about things, how they see things, hear things, smell things, taste things, touch things. This is your conscious mind. As the person makes decisions over and over or thinks about things over and over, those things move into your subconscious mind. This is where feelings are generated. Those feelings we refer to as spirit, and your spirit determines what the third plane does, your body.

I want to back up here just to make sure we're on the same page. The conscious mind is a thinking mind, the educated mind. The subconscious mind is the emotional mind, your spirit. The emotional mind determines the behavior we have or the actions the body is involved in. We have the ability to originate an image of what we would like our future to be like by impressing that picture upon the subconscious mind. Dr Thurman Fleet created this image, and it is called the genie. The genie allows us to have a picture to represent how our mind operates. The beautiful thing is you have the freedom to decide your thoughts, which determine your feelings, and then your feelings produce actions and behaviors, which finally produce your results. The reason it is called the genie is, like a genie, your mind will give you whatever you ask for. Now we have a picture we can use to help us have clarity of the picture of our mind. This is the genie.

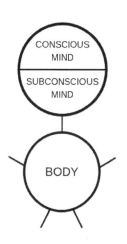

The genie is the secret. This is how people have become successful. If you think about something you've done and you become successful at, this is what you did. You took a thought and accepted it in your subconscious mind, then that thought created a feeling which was established in your subconscious mind, and that feeling created the action that your body took. Let's go back to a previous example. Athletes say at the end of the game what made them successful was their game plan and their preparation and being a total team player and everyone doing their part. What they actually did was accept a thought that they were going to win the championship, fell in love with the idea of that thought, and they didn't accept any other thought except that they were going to win. The body created actions according to the thought of winning, which gave the desired result.

The idea of winning that championship created a feeling and gave them a spirit which puts their body into action. Now, the only reason they did all the other things is because they accepted the thought first, that this is what was going to happen. Accepted a thought, it became a feeling, the body moved, and that's how we've gained ground on anything we've ever done. So, if you want people to change what they're doing, you're going to have to help them understand what's causing them to do what they're doing, and everything that's going on in the person's life is a direct reflection on what they're thinking about and what's going on inside, and we have the ability to choose that. The genie gives us a picture of our mind. When you are getting results in your life, good or bad, look at what you are telling the genie. Whatever the results are, they are based on what you were thinking.

Behaviors are the cause of the result, but are the secondary cause. You had to go to the primal cause, which was the spirit, the feeling, the subconscious mind, which is only controlled by your thinking and the thinking we put into it, and that's where we come up with the genie. The genie is the stick person. That is why it is on the front of the book. It's the secret, and every time you think of a result of something you want, you're going to think of the genie. You're going to think of the stick person, and you're going to ask yourself, "What was I thinking at that time? Because that determined my behavior, my spirit, which put my body into action." So now you know the secret to why and how you're accomplishing goals, and why you're getting or not getting results in your life. This idea changed everything for me. I finally figured out how I was getting or not getting results in my life. I talked about how I get whatever I want, and I didn't mean to be arrogant by that, but do you know why I get what I want? Because I understand the genie.

I understand what I think, what I convinced my subconscious mind of, is what my body is going to do, and I'm going to find a way to get what I want, and you can too. We've all had a crush before. Let's be honest. We've all had a first date with someone we really liked, and all we thought about was that person. You accepted a thought you really liked this person, and literally your heart would beat and race when you saw the person or when you thought about the person. Your body was taking action in an excited way. Your friends might have asked you, "What are you so happy about?" They could feel your happiness from 25 feet away. It's the genie. You couldn't tell anyone why you were doing that. "Oh, I'm in love," is what you would say.

Oh, okay. I'm in love. But really, you didn't know this at the time. The mind was just creating the feeling which put your body into action, and that's what the genie is, and this is the big secret. This is how you're going to start getting the results in your life you want. Now, of course, the Law of Polarity. We've talked about this before. Everything has its opposite. If something can be big, it can be small. If something can be hot, it can be cold. There is a negative to this also. That's why we call it the genie. The genie will give you what you tell it to give you, so if you accept a thought of anxiety about something, your subconscious mind is going to accept the thought of fear, and it's going to put your body in a feeling of nervousness. I've seen this happen to myself, where my body physically gets really hot. Results are not what we want.

Let's use the example of flying. Some people are frightened at the idea of flying. Now let's think of the genie. What is the thought that is going on initially? It's a scared or nervous thought. Then that thought created a feeling which comes over the body, and the body starts to do weird things. The body could cause shortness of breath, chest tightening, perhaps sweaty hands. The experience is torture. The body is physically producing actions which are not good. Then you look at the person beside you, on the same plane, and they are reading the newspaper, chewing gum. What are they telling their genie? The opposite of your genie, and the results are opposite. I am not saying it is easy to face your fears, but now you know where they come from.

The first time I ever publicly spoke in front of people I was a little nervous. I was prepared, but in my mind I'm saying to myself, *I hope I pull this off.* As I started to speak I got nervous, anxious, and incredibly hot under my collar and just couldn't wait for it to be over. It was a very short thing I had to speak about, but as I stopped I was literally sweating. I want you to understand how fast this can work. Your mind, your spirit, your body. I instantly got into a sweat, and my body was hot and anxious. This process can happen very fast, in a positive or negative aspect, so you have to be aware of that.

Another example: Let's say you saw a friend at the grocery store you haven't seen for five years. "Oh my gosh," you yell. You got really excited and you ran into the person and gave him a big hug. Your body started running within seconds of seeing the person. You had a thought, created a feeling, and the next thing you know you're running over to the person. It can happen that quickly, just like if you saw the professor from high school that told you you probably weren't going to do anything with your life. You instantly get a thought and feeling of anger, your body temperature increases, and you physically turn around and walk the other way: conscious mind, subconscious mind, body, and you went the other way. Things can happen quickly. Your mind is the most powerful thing on this entire planet, and I've just told you the secret on how to use it to your advantage.

Do not accept anything into your mind that is going to slow you down or is negative. Do not entertain any idea that does not propel you forward for what you want. Do not believe you can't have anything you want. You can tell your mind anything. The beautiful thing about your subconscious mind (and your spirit) is they are perfect. It only knows what you tell it. Whatever you tell your mind, it's going to grow, so we can tell it anything. It doesn't know the difference between what's real and what's imagined, so you have to practice telling yourself over and over and create the habit. If you want to fly private someday, then you tell yourself, "I'm going to fly private someday. I don't care what anyone tells me, the idea of flying private gets me excited, and I'll walk around here like I'm on this plane already. This is where the law of vibration comes into play.

We live in an ocean of motion. The world's turning, energy is all around us. There are cameras, Kirlian photography, that can film the energy leaving your body, so we know energy is all around us, and that's what the Law of Vibration is. What you tell yourself and how you feel determines your energy. Most people have heard of the Law of Attraction, but it's the secondary law. The Law of Vibration determines what you attract. So, if I'm telling myself I can hit this goal, or maybe we don't have enough manpower to grow this team, then my feeling or my vibration is going to go out and attract a winning result or a losing result. The Law of Vibration determines what's attracted into your life. That's why it's so important you focus on serving others and finding the good in people and giving people compliments and encouraging them. Every time you do that it keeps your vibration attracting more positive to you, and that's the way we want to live.

You have to watch your vocabulary—instead of saying the negative to something, say the positive. Keep all the negative out of your thinking and out of your life. Remember from the paradigms, what we think about determines the feelings we have, and those feelings are what puts our bodies into action. I've learned to love the genie, and I want you to love the genie, too. My kids understand the genie. I ask them each day what they are telling their genie. They tell me it's going to be an amazing day. Think about something you did in your past that was really awesome. Maybe you went to a state championship, graduated from high school, graduated from college, maybe you got that award you were trying to get... I want you to go back to when you started. I guarantee you it started with positive thoughts. Now, initially you might say, "Well, this is going to be challenging." That doesn't mean you don't believe you can do it. But it started with the thought of what it would be like to hold that trophy or to hold that championship or to achieve that goal you wanted. And that's where it started. The genie. You told the genie, "This is what I want. And the genie went to work producing the feelings of that set goal, and then your body did the work. People do this all the time. The difference between people who are successful and people who aren't is they make a habit out of doing habits that are beneficial to personal growth.

And you know why? Because they have a spirit about something they want. That's why they do it. They want something, and that's why they go and get it. They obsess and dream about it, and the feeling they have, they can't get rid of until they hit the goal because they've convinced their thinking mind, the conscious mind and the subconscious mind, they can have it. And once you've convinced the thought, the feeling generates, and it's over. Game over. You're going to hit your goal every time.

We gave you an image of the genie. That's the mind. That is how your mind operates. Keying into your conscious mind determines your spirit and feeling, and your subconscious mind moves your body. The genie, the genie, the genie... I said that three times because I want you to remember the genie. And now you know the secret. Let's look at a picture of what happens to us as we use the genie.

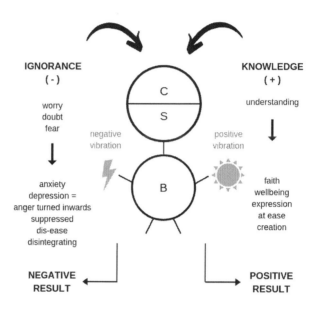

Every problem in the world is factored around one thing: ignorance. Ignorance means you just don't know something or lack knowledge. It has nothing do with intelligence. In this image you can see as we go through life being ignorant to things or unaware that causes us to worry, and then we start to doubt things in our life. That in turn causes fear and anxiety, which lead to depression. Depressions is anger turned inward, and we suppress those feelings. This causes the body to be at dis-ease and to disintegrate over time. The vibration was always in a negative state and ends up attracting a negative result. As you can see on the left side of the image.

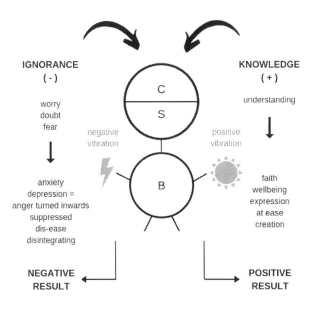

Let's look at the right side. The only way to fix ignorance is study. When you gain knowledge on things you have a better understanding on that subject. We should study our entire life. It feels amazing to know things you didn't know before. As that understanding builds your perception changes and you build a faith about things. This faith creates wellbeing and a body that expresses itself, and you release energy. This is a body that is at ease and a body that is creating and moving forward. The vibration in this case, I used a sunshine, is positive or flowing, which attracts positive results. Now you have the knowledge the next time you don't know something you can change it and you can see what your mind and body are doing when we have negative and positive thoughts.

The next time you're not getting a result you want, you're going to know why. Now you have accountability, which is a great thing because now you can't blame anyone else for why you're not hitting your goals. You are the genie. The genie will give whatever you ask it. It's up to you to ask and move forward.

6

SETTING REAL GOALS!

If you asked 100 people walking down the sidewalk if they knew what their goals were, how many do you think will have goals? Hardly any. If you happen to find a couple that had goals and you ask them if they had those goals written down, how many do you think would have them actually written down? Almost none of them would have their goals written down.

We're going to talk about getting everything you want out of your life, which comes in the form of setting goals. Setting goals, and goals in general, can be a tricky topic. There's a lot of people that have their opinions on goals.

At this point it is important to understand the Law of Perpetual Transmutation. We will discuss the laws in Chapter Seven, but we need to discuss this one now. The Law of Perpetual Transmutation. Sounds like a lot of jumbled words there, but let me explain what that means. This is defined as energy that moves into physical form. Thoughts can produce tangible things. The images you have in your mind most often materialize in the results of life, so if you think negative, then what's going to materialize as a result is most likely negative.

Likewise, if you think positive and have positive thoughts, what's going to most often materialize is positive. What you visualize in your mind equals your results. Energy moves into physical form, so there is energy flowing to and through us constantly. We're in an ocean of motion. The world is turning. As you sit still and lay in your bed at night, falling asleep, you are still moving. There is still energy all around you. It's moving to and through us. Simian Kirlian perfected a camera that can take a picture of energy leaving your body, so we know energy is real. We want to use this energy in our favor.

I want to introduce you to a way to reach the goals you really want to hit in life. Something big in your life. A goal that is powerful and puts your dreams into reality.

In order to learn how to do what you're about to do, I'm going to have to ask you to use your imagination. It is one of your higher mental faculties. We used to dream and imagine things when we were little kids. As we got older we were taught to be logical and stop daydreaming and get to work. In essence, we are taught at a young age that maybe imagination isn't that important, or that it is for little kids—but it's very important. Since we can have anything we want in this life, and I mean anything, we have to start imagining. I want you to build an image and then live in that image. Whatever it is you're trying to get to, I want you to build that image, a mental picture, and we're going to do that today together, and then I want you to start living in that image as if you have it right now. We just discussed in the previous chapter how we think in pictures. Without your imagination there can be no creation in your life. What that means is someone else will always be the star in your movie. We don't want anyone else to be the star in our movie. It's our life, or as I say, "It's my dream. Stay out of my dream." Remember, everything is created twice: first in thought with your imagination, your mind; second when it manifests into your material world. Everything is started with a thought. Everything that ever was and ever will be started with someone's thought.

Positive thought equals positive feeling, which equals positive action. Imagine you have access to all the resources you'll ever need and you can have anything you want. All I want you to do is clearly define what you want, which most people don't. They get so locked up with limitations they can never go to this place, so I want you to forget all that for a little bit. Forget time, money, resources, and especially forget this silly word: logic. Logic never got us to the moon, logic never got us in flight. Thank goodness the Wright Brothers didn't use logic. Alex Honnold didn't use logic when he became the only man to climb El Capitan without a rope. Logic never got a sub four-minute mile. You must believe there's going to be zero growth beyond the beliefs that you have. If you don't believe, there will be no growth. Don't let the idea that it is not logical to have the goal you want. Lose that word in our vocabulary.

If you attempt to accomplish something beyond the belief that you have, your mind will quickly create ideas and reasons why it can't be done, so we're going to use our imagination to get us what we want. Imagination is a higher mental faculty which helps us go beyond our normal views of life.

Let's discuss the three types of goals: A, B, and C goals

"A" Goals

These are goals you already know how to hit. You're basically ruling out any creativity or imagination. If you are counting on motivation from a goal you have already hit before, it's not going to happen. For example, if your goal is to get a new truck and you have a truck now you bought new, then you already know how to get a new truck. There is little motivation in going after something you have already done. It will cause little excitement. You're not getting out of bed every morning to go and hit a goal you already know how to hit. Especially when you have already had the feeling of driving a new truck. I need you to dream again like you did as a little kid—and I mean really dream. Imagine you can have anything you want—anything.

"B" Goals

This is a goal you _think_ you can do. Someone inspired you to do something and you got some motivation. Since the idea wasn't really yours there is lack of follow through. You have an idea, but as soon as the plan has issues you abort the mission and the goal is no longer on the radar.

"C" Goals

This is where you have to get involved with your creative process, your imagination, and begin to build a fantasy. This is a goal you have never done and one that you have no idea how you are going to accomplish initially. Don't let that keep you from setting the goal. Just write it down. The goal is big enough when you shake your head and laugh at it with disbelief. That is how you know you are setting the right goal. Some examples, I want to own an NFL team, a 100-foot yacht, the ability to fly private with your family and friends, having a beach house, a ski house and a home-base house. Starting a charity that can help the entire world. Having 100 million dollars in your account. It doesn't matter, just write it down. Remember, not many billionaires started out as a billionaire. They built something over time.

I had the luxury of having lunch with Mark Cuban at The Palm Restaurant in Dallas many years ago. I asked him many questions that day. One of them was, "How did you know you were going to be a billionaire?" He told me he didn't know he was going to be a billionaire, but he loved computers and basketball. He was trying to figure out a way to listen to the basketball games through the computer. Those were his passions. Mark and his team sold broadcast.com to yahoo for a billion dollars. Mark knew he wanted to make something amazing with his computer business. I didn't ask Mark, but I bet if I could ask him if he wanted to be massively successful before he was, I am guessing he would have said yes. Just a hunch. I could be wrong. Sir Edmond Hilary once said, "You don't just wonder around and find yourself on top of Mount Everest, you have to plan it." You need to dream it, see it, believe it, study it, obsess about it. Once again, you don't need to know how you are going to get there, but you do need to know what you want. The how doesn't come in to play until you decide to go after what you want. Once you get in harmony with what you are passionate about, then the Law of Perpetual Transmutation starts to work. It can happen for you too. Don't let those negative thoughts keep you from reaching the goals you have always wanted. Remember, everything you see around you was once an idea, conceived in the imagination.

Airplanes were a fantasy, the automobile was a fantasy, the internet was a fantasy, and you mentally begin to play with that fantasy until it starts to take effect and you start to take it seriously, then you flip-flop from using your imagination and start using your reasoning ability, another one of your higher intellectual factors, and then begin to build an idea more clearly, which is where you turn your fantasy into a theory and then a goal. But before we can do that, before we start with the fantasy and turn it into a theory, we must ask two important things. Am I willing? Am I able? Here is how it starts. As you can see in this image, we start with a fantasy, and over time as we repeat the goal card we continue to put that image on the screen in our mind, and it becomes a theory. Theory is when you have convinced yourself you are going to do it, and then it physically happens in your life as the goal.

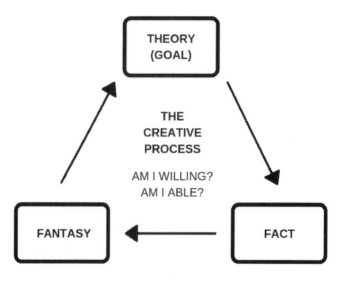

The first question is, "Am I able to do this?" If we consider the only two sources of reference, science and theology, both clearly indicate potential is infinite. So the answer to that question is yes, of course you're able to do this.

The second question, you ask, "Am I willing?" The answer is yes! Once you made the conscious decision, you are willing and you are able, the Law of Perpetual Transmutation will come into play. The law states energy moves into physical form. The image you hold in your mind most often materializes and results in your life. So this law takes over, and your goal begins to move into physical form with and through you. It causes your behaviors to change while at the same time attracting all things required to reach your goal. Before long the theory becomes a fact. Einstein said, "Everything is energy, and that is all there is to it. Match the frequency of the reality you want, and you cannot help but get that reality. It can be no other way. This is not philosophy, this is physics." Get in touch with the reality of what you want and get in harmony with that energy. It can be no other way. Stop worrying if you will have enough time or money. Stop worrying about the resources. There's infinite resources available to you. You don't need the money or time until you make the decision to do it. Once you do you will see the resources start to show up. Trust me. The "C" goal once again is one you have never done before and one that starts with a fantasy. This type of goal will get you jumping out of bed every day, You're excited either creating something or you're going backward. You're disintegrating, and who wants to disintegrate? No one wants to go backward, so we need to create something that gets us excited. Now, let's talk about how we get this done. I want to talk about a goal card. A goal card is the size of a business card or an index card. It's something you're going to write your "C" goal on, and I typically have a one-year goal and a two to four-year goal on my goal card. Here is an image to help you. You can write on both sides.

MY GOAL _____ **20**____
I'm so happy and grateful now that...

_____ ...and I love it!

This is the same process as when we are changing paradigms. We want to write the "C" goal in the present tense, as if you have it already. Remember, your subconscious mind doesn't know what is real or imagined. It is like the earth, and it will grow whatever you plant in it. We want our subconscious mind to think you are there already, and it will start to move things into motion to complete the goal.

I'm so happy and grateful now that I'm a millionaire, and I love it. And then you're going to fold it in half and carry this card around with you. Everywhere you go. I keep mine in my pocket every day.

I'm so happy and grateful now that I'm flying private, and I love it. I'm so happy and grateful now that I live in my dream house, and I love it. I am so happy and grateful now that I am running my own business. I am so happy and grateful I am able to serve others in a charity. I am so happy and grateful I am able to buy my first home. I am so happy and grateful I am starting my own business. I am so happy and grateful I am writing my first book/blog. I am so happy and grateful I am running my first marathon.

Every time you touch this card it puts a picture on your mind's eye and sends a light message to your brain, and a picture will come onto the screen in your mind. We think in pictures. Every time you touch that goal card you picture whatever's on that goal card in your mind. We have already established that everything ever started with a thought then becomes a reality. We have to get the "C" goal in your mind, and that is what the goal card does. We are auto-suggesting the goal to our subconscious mind the same as when we were changing the paradigms. Remember, the same rules apply when you use the goal card as when changing a paradigm.

Just to review:

Rule One: We must start our new idea with gratitude and in the present tense, which is why we say, "I am so happy and grateful now that…" If you are not grateful for what you have you will not attract anything more. Not in the future, not in the past, right here and right now. Live in the picture you created in your mind until it happens.

Rule Two: You need to say your new idea out loud, as there is vibrations in your voice, and those vibrations determine what you attract.

Rule Three: Have faith in what you are reading. If you just read it and don't believe things will change, then the exercise is pointless.

Rule Four: Concentrate when you read it.

Rule Five: Repeat your idea as many times in a day as you can.

I want to give you an example. I was a young manager back in 2001 and was doing field sales and passed by a travel agency where I saw this really cool magazine in the window. On the magazine cover was a photo of a hut in the middle of the ocean in the middle of the crystal-clear blue water. As I opened the magazine I saw the inside of what the hut looked like, and it had a glass floor in the middle of it. The place was called Tahiti. I promised myself I would experience this photograph. So, I kept the magazine and put it on my coffee table in my office.

Just plant the seed. Put the picture of the goal on the screen in your mind. That's what the goal card does. Obsess about the goal card and let the rest of it take care of itself. Now, I wanted to go to Tahiti in 2001. I didn't have the money or time to go to Tahiti when I set the goal. This is when most people let logic ruin everything. "Hey, don't set a goal because how could I when I don't have the time or money to do something?"

I saw the goal and thought about it all the time. I dreamed about what it would be like to swim in the clear blue water. I smiled every time I thought about it. People would go by my coffee table in my office and ask me where that was. I told them, and I told them I was going to go there. It didn't happen until 2006. I just knew at some point it was going to happen. Your goals don't know time, so don't get frustrated. If you get frustrated and subject yourself back to the negative thinking and paradigms, you might as well grab your goal card, tear it up, and throw it away. You're now digging up all of the seeds you planted in your subconscious. Don't do that. Your goals will manifest when the time is right. This is the Law of Gender, which states everything has a digestion period, and goals will manifest when the time is right.

Just because you have a goal card doesn't mean you can go and sit on your couch and wait for it to happen. You have to take massive action and steps toward reaching your goal in understanding of the law.

The biggest reason people are frustrated with their goal card is the goal is not big enough, and they're frustrated because when they read it they're basically reading frustration because they're reading something that isn't exciting them. You're going to continue to attract frustration into your life until you put massive goals on your goal card. Something you really, really want. And you know why we don't put massive things on goal cards? Our good old friend the paradigm. Deep inside, as you write it, you think this will never happen, so you end up writing something on your goal card that is basically nothing or logical.

I want you guys to understand how powerful these things are. Let me give you an example. Jim Carrey wrote a check to himself many years ago for $10,000,000 for services rendered, and he carried this check around with him everywhere he went. Jim signed for *Dumb and Dumber* for $7,000,000. Not quite 10 million, but he was well on his way, and way past that now. He should've wrote $50 million on the check, because he would've gotten that. Think about your goal.

Forget about what your family thinks about your goal. Write it down or speak it into existence every day.

The exciting news about this process is you have already done it before. That's right, you have already done this before, you just didn't have the goal card at the time. Let me explain. There has been a time in your life when you really wanted something. A Matchbox car, a Barbie doll, a new baseball bat, a college degree, to play on the varsity team, to fly first class, and the list goes on and on. Let's walk you through the process. You had a thought, you put the picture in your mind, you thought about it and talked about it every day. You imagined doing or using that particular thing in the present, as if you already had it, and then guess what happened? That's right...you got it! You achieved the goal. Take a minute and think back to something you have already done that was big. If you walk yourself through the process you will not have to take my word for it, you can take your own word for it. The goal card puts the use of your physical touch on the goal to help you keep it on your mind more easily.

We have to trick our subconscious mind, because the subconscious mind is going to grow whatever you put in there. We're planting the seeds, but when we get frustrated and we read goals we've already hit, we're basically digging up those seeds and they're not planning anymore.

The goal card will keep you excited because you know you're going to eventually attain your goals.

7

DOING THINGS A CERTAIN WAY

There is a science to building wealth and fulfillment, and it's an exact science. Like algebra or arithmetic, it is exact. There are certain laws which govern the process of acquiring wealth and fulfillment. Once you learn, live, and practice these laws, you will build wealth and fulfillment with certainty. The good thing about these laws is if you use these laws, consciously or unconsciously, you will build wealth and fulfillment. In other words, if you don't even realize you are using them you will build wealth and fulfillment. My guess is you are already using some of them.

There is one great law, energy. Energy is physical and mental. Mental science is based on this one great law, and there's some subsidiary laws which coordinate or operate with energy. We're going to get into all the different laws, but the best definition of the natural laws seems to be it's a uniform and orderly method of God. Now, from a theological standpoint, that would be God is in control of the universe. From a science perspective, it's energy. There's energy all around us; energy is constantly flowing to and through us.

Albert Einstein said, "Everything is energy, and that's all there is to it. Match the frequency of the reality you want, and you cannot help but get that reality. It can be no other way. This is not philosophy, this is physics."

There's a scientific standpoint on the universe, the laws, and unlike any other form of animal life that has been created, we were given the power of choice, freewill. Along with this comes responsibility, and we have to be aware of that. The capacity to choose does not involve freedom from the consequence of our choice, but the laws or rules which govern every individual, and which we covered to some degree so far, are exact. These are the laws that govern the material universe. Now, once again, you can choose to act in accordance with these laws or you can disregard them, but you can't alter them in any way, and these laws forever operate and hold you to a strict accountability.

There is not the slightest allowance made for ignorance just because you don't know what they are. Once again, it doesn't matter if you follow these laws unconsciously or consciously, you will get the results. The Law of Attraction will deliver to you what you do not want as quickly as it will deliver to you what you do want. The ownership of money and property comes as a result of doing things a certain way and not doing a certain thing. Fulfillment and wealth come from doing things a certain way, which is what we're talking about. Those who do things in a certain way, whether on purpose or accident, are going to build wealth and be fulfilled, and just the same, those who do not do things in a certain way will not have the results over time they desire.

Getting wealthy and having fulfillment is not a matter of environment.

Some environments may be more favorable than others. When you have two people in the same business or in the same neighborhood and one gets wealthy while the other doesn't, it indicates getting wealthy is a result of doing things a certain way. The ability to do things a certain way is not due solely to talent, because many people who have great talent remain poor, while others who have very little talent are wealthy.

With all these things we've talked about so far, we must come to the conclusion that building wealth and fulfillment is a result of doing things a certain way.

Once again, remember talented people build wealth and fulfillment, blockheads build wealth and fulfillment, and intellectually brilliant people build wealth and fulfillment. Think it, feel it, do it, and you will attract it. This is the great secret of life. Think it, feel it, do it, and you will attract it.

The Law of Perpetual Transmutation. We have discussed this before, but this is defined as energy that moves into physical form. The image you have in your mind most often materializes in the results in life. So, if you think negative, then what's going to materialize as results is most likely negative. Likewise, if you think positive and have positive thoughts, what's going to most often materialize is positive. What you visualize in your mind equals your results. Energy moves into physical form, so there is energy constantly flowing to and through us. You have to understand your energy, how you're vibrating. What's going on is going to materialize into the results in your life.

It's impossible. I can't do it. Your thinking mind is the most powerful force in the entire world, and remember, your mind is in every part of your body. The power of thought is the most powerful thing in the entire planet. What you think controls your body, so if you want to change, give serious thought to what you think about, because you become what you think about.

Does it make sense we can think about failure, doubt, poverty, disease, and attract wealth, success, health? Does that make any sense? No, it doesn't make any sense. These laws are to help you become aware of what's going on and what you actually think about. The most powerful thing in the entire planet, the thinking mind, is at your disposal.

It's extremely important you understand what's going on and what you think about. Think about an electrician, for example. An electrician could really hurt him or herself if not aware of how powerful electricity can be. So, electricians study it, understand it. They understand how conduction works and conductors and all the positives and negatives that go along with electricity. And when they understand how powerful it is, that it could really hurt them, they can channel the electricity in a way that is in their benefit because their understanding of the power of electricity.

This is the same thing with the Law of Thinking. We have access to an amazing power source, the power of thought. When you get in harmony with how much power you have, with the way you think, you will have an amazing advantage in your life. This is how we're going to start to do things in a certain way that builds wealth and fulfillment. When you're thinking positive and thinking abundance and generosity, then you are going to start to move toward those things. We need to use the power of thinking to help grow.

The Law of Vibration. Law of vibration is in harmony with The Law of Attraction. Everything vibrates, nothing rests. Conscious awareness of vibration is called feeling. So, the Law of Vibration is becoming aware of your feelings. Your thoughts control your paradigms and your vibrations, which will dictate what you attract.

Again, conscious awareness of vibration is called feeling. So become aware of how your feeling on a daily basis. If I'm vibrating negative because I'm thinking negative, then I'm going to attract negative and I'm going to build habits that aren't the ones I want. So, when you're not feeling good, become aware of what you're thinking, then think something pleasant. Your vibration determines what the Law of Attraction goes and gets for you. Become aware of how you are feeling. Not feeling that great today? No problem, no one does every day. But just tell yourself, "I'm happy, healthy, wealthy." We don't want to attract things into our life that have a negative impact on us from negative thoughts. Let's become aware of how these two laws work together.

The Law of Relativity. Nothing is good or bad, big or small, until you relate it to something. This is one I use a lot, and you might too. Practice relating your situation, briefly, to something much worse, and yours will always look amazing. I'm going to grab a paperclip in my office. All right, now I want you to ask you, is this paper clip big or small? And some of you might be inclined to say it's small. Alright, now I am grabbing my cell phone. Now, the cell phone I'm holding is much bigger than the paperclip. In this case the paper clip is small. When I compare the paperclip to the tip of my pen, the paper clip is much bigger. In this case the paperclip is big. So the paperclip can be big or small depending on what we're comparing it to.

When problems arise in your life, you want to focus on if the problem is as big as we are making it, or is it not that big of a deal. If something's going wrong or upsetting you or frustrating you, compare your situation, briefly, to someone who has it much worse. I often pass people at the stoplights where I live, and they are asking for money, and when I see those people who have very little, I remember my problems are small.

Let's focus and practice relating our situation to something much worse, briefly, and yours will always look amazing—that is the Law of Relativity. What are you comparing your situation to? When you compare it to something that's much worse, you're going to stay in that good state. You're going to get back to being a solution-oriented person figuring out what you can do to move forward, and that's the Law of Relativity.

The next law we want to discuss is the Law of Polarity. The Law of Polarity states everything has an opposite. Hot, cold; up, down; good, bad. If it's ten feet for me to walk across the room in my office, it must be ten feet back across the room back to my chair. Everything has an opposite. If something can be hot, then it can be cold. If you live in Chicago or you live somewhere cold in the winter, the lakes are frozen, and in the summer they're unfrozen. So what we want to do with the Law of Polarity is constantly look for the good in people and situations. Because if something can be bad, then it can be good.

Funerals are not fun. That's the worst when you lose someone you love. But if something can be bad, it can be good. Well, what's the good? What do people talk about? At funerals they talk about how the person is not suffering anymore, they're in a better place, and they lived a great life. They try to find all of the amazing aspects to the person, because the person's not there anymore. And the Law of Polarity is used in this case, because in a bad situation there can be good. And that's the most familiar example I can use that people know. Don't get me wrong, losing someone is the worst. This law is just trying to help us get back to the positive as quickly as we can so we stay in a good vibration.

The problem is we rarely look for the good in situations. When bad happens we just focus on the bad, and when we focus on the bad, guess what? We get more of it. We get more bad because our vibration is in a negative state. So, constantly look for the good in people and in situations. This takes some practice, especially when people get to us. Let's remember, it's not about them it's about you staying in control and staying in a positive vibration. You don't have to, but if you want to build wealth and fulfillment, this is the science and these are the laws. We want to focus on the good. That's the Law of Polarity. I see many people who use this law. It is probably the most common one I see people using, and I am guessing they don't even know it. It doesn't matter, it still is working in your favor.

The next law I want to focus on is the Law of Non-Resistance.

This means what we resist exists. So when you're trying to avoid a problem in your life, when you keep focusing on that problem or the person that's causing the problem, they're going to continue to exist in your life. So what we have to do is learn to respond. We don't want to react to things, we want to respond. We don't want to let people get us out of our good attitudes or good vibrations. We don't want to fight back. We want to just let it go. Once again, not reacting, only responding.

Remember when you were a kid and someone did something mean to you? Your first inclination was to get them back. I would guess most of us were taught "if someone did something to you that was mean, then you get them back." The problem is many things, but mainly that this cycle goes on and on.

When resistance comes, just let it go. For example, when a small creek is flowing from the mountains and is becoming a big river, initially the little creek doesn't have much power, so when it runs into a force of resistance, a rock or a tree, it just slowly finds a route around the rock or the tree and continues to keep going, and that's how eventually it picks up momentum. It merges with another stream and eventually becomes more of a creek. And the creek merges with the river and the river becomes a river like the Mighty Mississippi. The Mississippi doesn't start out large, it starts out as a little creek with resistance. Now, if the creek had met resistance and stopped it would never become the mighty river it is, and it's the same thing with problems in your life. Stop resisting people that bother you. Just respond to them. If someone wants to bring a problem to you, just respond, don't react. Just keep moving. We don't want to resist anything in our life, because as we keep resisting it is going to keep existing. When resistance comes up, just let it go.

Reacting is a habit, as is responding. But responding means you actually have to think before you do or say something. Reacting, you just say the first thing that comes up a lot of time, which is not a good thing.

There is someone or a person that is bothering you and you keep thinking about this person and you keep resisting this person, and funny thing is that person keeps showing up in your life. There they are again, and that's because you're thinking about that person, and what you think about you attract in life, and as you learn more about these laws all of this will making sense to you. When you are resisting, that is not a vibration you want to be in. When you are fighting back or angry at someone or something, that is not a vibration you want to be in. Remember, how we vibrate determines what we attract.

If you're in debt, stop resisting debt. Just respond and go. Start focusing on abundance now. I'm not worried about debt. I'm not worried about my company. I'm not worried about my situation. I'm going to respond with an attitude of abundance and positivity, and I'm going to think about the things I want versus resisting the things in my life that I don't want. And that is the Law of Nonresistance.

The Law of Increase is all about sending out good energy to anyone or anything you can. Send loving energy out in the form of praise. The more you praise, the better things are and the better things become in your life, and it works in everything in your life. If you want to increase anything in your life, you have to praise it, praise what you have. The two words that are most missed in many things are "thank you." This is a form of praise, and is a habit you want to attract in your life. The Law of Increase gives praise to someone or a certain situation, because the more you send out positive energy the more you stay in a vibration of positive energy. And it feels good to give someone a compliment or tell them thank you for a good job.

With the Law of Increase, we want to focus on prosperity and helping and serving. In this world, serving is how you're going to build wealth and fulfillment. It feels good to serve. It feels good to give a compliment, but this is one you're going to have to really focus on, because in order to give a true compliment it has to come from inside. And if you're not feeling good on the inside, it's very tough to give a compliment, very tough to give praise. It's very tough to increase someone else's life when inside you're not feeling good. Once again, there is a science to building wealth and fulfillment, and this is one of the major laws. Focus on praising the things you have in your life. Focus on praising other people that you work with. And I don't mean unwarranted praise or flattery. I mean, if someone does something good, say something good to them—and that doesn't mean just walking around giving people compliments that aren't warranted or they haven't earned. You want to praise the people that do great things around you, which builds comradery and trust with them in you. You want to praise the things you have in the form of gratitude, because if you're not grateful for the things you have, you will not attract any more things into your life. If you're not grateful for the people in your life, you will not attract any more friends or special people in your life. And once again, these all tie together, because when we're sending out praise we're focusing on being in a positive state, not negative. Tell people the good you see in them and say thank you as many times in a day as you can.

The Law of Gender allows us to understand the seeds we are planting have a growth period. Your ideas are seeds and will move into form and physical results. Be patient, your goals will manifest when the time is right. Just trust that they will. If you don't hit your goal by a certain date, just keep going. When you build the image in your mind, a definite period of time must elapse before that image turns into a physical thing. The harvest is coming, just keep moving toward it.

The Law of Rhythm deals with the timing of things. There are good times and there are bad. Each year, after fall comes winter. The tide at the beach goes out and comes back in. In life, when you are on a downswing, do not feel bad. It's not always easy, but just know that, like the tide, those down times will change. We want to focus on the good times to come, which will allow the good times to be attracted faster.

Whatever you send out into the universe comes back to you, and that is what the Law of Cause and Effect is about. Your actions and reactions are opposite and equal. We want to treat everyone with respect and say good things to everyone. What you send out to them will come back to you. Every effect must have a cause, and in turn every cause must have an effect. We are all interested in results. Results in our physical health, relationships, the respect you earn and the material income we attract. Now, you may focus on some of these more than others. When we take care of our bodies, our physical and mental health, the effect is our bodies take care of us. When you maintain close contact with your most important relationships, the effect is those relationships are there for you. The better I treat everyone, not just some, the effect is the respect you are granted. The better ways you find to serve others, the effect is your material income will increase. Never worry about what you are going to get, just focus on what you can give. Focus on the cause and the effect will automatically take care of itself. Which means we need to make the cause positive.

My favorite name for a law, the Vacuum Law of Prosperity. Nature abhors a vacuum. If you want to bring new things or ideas into your life you have to make room for them. Try this: go into your closet and give away all the old clothes you don't wear anymore. Watch and see if you don't have new clothes in there in no time. You might say to yourself, "Well, Michael, I will just go out and buy new clothes." It doesn't matter where the clothes come from, the point is you have new clothes you would have never gotten if you had not made room for them. Make room in your life for greatness, thoughts, and ideas. Get rid of the things in your life you don't need and that are clogging up your life. This could be anything: people, furniture, clothes, negative ideas or thoughts.

Last but definitely not least is the Law of Forgiveness. We need to forgive those in our past who have hurt us. We also need to forgive ourselves for people we have hurt. Carrying around negative vibrations about people who have hurt us or we have hurt is not going to help you get ahead. Guilt and anger are very serious paradigms that slow us down. Forgive that person in your high school for what they did to you. Forgive the guy or girl who broke your heart. Forgive yourself for what you said or did to that person. It is in the past and we need to move on from it. We have all been hurt and all hurt others before. We are all, including me, a work in progress.

Forgiving is a cleansing process that clears out all of the negative we carry. It's not about the other person, it is about you. If you did something wrong to someone else and they forgave you, then that does nothing for you, but does for them. We are talking about you cleaning out the negative. The Law of Forgiveness is about letting go forever. Say out loud that you forgive whatever it is you need to forgive, and let it go forever. You might not feel like you should be forgiven, but you should. You are worthy.

Remember these laws are exact and cannot be changed or modified. If you want to build wealth and fulfillment, you must live and implement these laws.

These laws have changed my life, and they're going to help you change your life.

8

WHAT IS SUCCESS, AND THE ONE KEY TO IT

There are many opinions about success. What's it mean? Have I accomplished it? Many questions revolve around this, so we're going to clear this up. Make sure you know success is a law, and just like any of the laws we talk about, we're going to break it down for you so you have a better understanding and hopefully feel better about what it means to be successful. Raymond Holliwell said, "He who thinks he can, can." God intended for every man and woman to succeed and enjoy every good in the Universe. I think that's interesting, because I think sometimes people think, *Well, does that mean me?* Yes, it means you. Everyone has the ability to enjoy success, and each person is endowed with a set of higher faculties: reason, will, imagination, intuition, memory, and perception.

We've talked about these before. We have our five sensory faculties: see, hear, smell, taste, touch. Every person on earth contains within them the capacity for endless development. Advancement into all things is what the Law of Success is all about. development and moving forward should be the aim for everyone.

It's important you follow the process of advancement, and when we think about the process of advancement and success, we're going to use the example of Mother Nature. All the processes of nature are successful. Think about that for a second. There's not anything nature does that's not successful. Nature knows no failures, and she never planned anything but success. All of nature's processes are planned for success. Nature never intends on failing. Nature aims at results in every form and manner, so we have to use nature's example in order to achieve success. Think of a tree growing, a hurricane, a blizzard, a field of corn for a second. When nature starts the process it intends on completion or success. A tree or a storm doesn't stop halfway or give up because it got lazy. It plans to go until completion, and it is going to do whatever it was planning to do. It keeps moving forward until the desired goal is complete. As long as you plan to keep moving forward and never give up on your progress, then you're modeling advancement after Mother Nature, and you can do this to discover all the secrets to success. We also have the ability to develop an intelligence in any area, and that will solve most of life's mysteries.

Success is about advancing. Are you advancing? Are you moving forward? If you are advancing and improving your life and others around you, then you are successful. Moving forward for advancement is success.

Now, you can stand still or you can go backward, but both of these are going to diminish any chances you have of success, the reason being we don't have the spirit of advancement when we're standing still, and then we're going backward. We're either creating or disintegrating, and creating in this case would be a form of advancement. Creating the study you want to do, creating the personal development you want to do, creating the knowledge you want to attain, creating the vision you want—all are moving you forward, which by the law is success. It doesn't matter what field you're advancing in. The more you develop that mindset, the better chance of succeeding. We have to convince ourselves that "we can" do anything. We have to fall in love with the spirit of "I can," and this is the key to a successful attitude. Modern psychology has discovered the person who thinks he or she can, will speedily develop the power that can persistently develop your mind. It won't be long before you're actually doing what you want to do. Discover that if you convince yourself you can, you're going to start developing this power quickly and persistently develop your skillset to move into success and advance, ultimately becoming successful. The Law of Success is about the advancing person.

So, how in the world are we supposed to understand this defining key for success when most of us aren't even aware of what this major key is? Learning what it is, is only the first step, then we have to develop an ability to use it as a whole other process. What we're about to do is make you fully aware of what the key to success is and help you understand how to use it. I hope I've built enough impulse. Hopefully you're ready for this defining key for success.

The key is decision. Since this key is not taught in schools or in most companies, once again, the individual is expected to develop this mental ability. And you have to do it on your own.

You can eliminate conflict and confusion in your life by becoming proficient at making decisions, and with decision-making brings order to your mind, and of course this order is reflected in your results, and a person who fails to develop their ability to make decisions is really doomed, because indecision sets up internal conflicts, and those conflicts can escalate into mental and emotional battles within yourself. It all starts with decision. Psychiatrists have a name to describe these internal wars people battle within their minds on not being able to make a decision, and that term is ambivalence. Ambivalence tells us one person can have opposite feelings toward the same objective.

We have this objective, which coexists in one person, and we have opposite feelings toward that objective. You can see how this would bring confusion and an unsettling feeling. In other words, there's one objective in your mind, and you have the opposite feeling toward that objective. There's a very basic law of the Universe. We've talked about it before. It's create or disintegrate indecision causes disintegration. How often have you heard a person say, "I don't know what to do?" How often have you heard yourself say, "What should I do?" "Should I stay or go?" Everyone on occasion has experienced these feelings of ambivalence, and the cause of ambivalence, once again, is indecision. But it's deeper than just indecision. Indecision is the cause of ambivalence. However, it's a secondary cause, not the primary cause, and it's been proven in studying behavior of people who have become very proficient at making decisions have one thing in common: confidence in themselves.

Insecurity in yourself is a habit, and this is a paradigm that slows you down, so you can start to change the habit through auto suggestion that you're so happy and grateful now that you're strong, confident, and you make great decisions on a daily basis and you love it. You need to convince yourself you actually are good at making decisions. Making decisions is a habit.

Decide right where you are with whatever you have. That's it. That is the principle of decision making, and it's precisely why most people never master this important aspect of life. They permit their resources to dictate if and when a decision will or can be made, and they let the appearance and resources determine if and when they can make a decision.

Once you make the decision you will find all the people, resources, and ideas you need. Every single time.

Whatever you need to achieve your goal, you will attract, but you will only attract it once you make the decision. Now, there's many people who will say it's crazy, you can't just decide to do something if you do not have the necessary resources, and that's fine if that's the way they choose to think, but that's a very limited way of thinking, and in truth is probably not even thinking at all and is very likely an opinion being expressed that was inherited from another member of their family who didn't think either. And, as we discussed before, you're thinking mind is the most powerful thing in the entire Universe.

Decision makers are great thinkers. There's a very select few people who actually attempt to control their thoughts. We have to realize thought ultimately controls every decision we make, and we are the sum total of our thoughts, and by taking charge this very minute, can guarantee a good day and a good life and refuse to let unhappy, negative people or circumstances affect us. The biggest issue you'll encounter when making important decisions in your life is circumstance, and we let circumstance get us off the hook when we should be giving everything we've got. More dreams and goals are lost because of circumstance than any other single factor.

How often have you caught yourself saying, "Yeah, I'd like to do that or have this, but I can't because..." And then whatever you fill in the blank with after that is basically because of the circumstance. Circumstances may cause a detour in your life, but you can never permit them to stop you from making important decisions, and you should decide today that you make the circumstances, circumstances do not make you. The next time you hear someone say they would like to go on a vacation or purchase a car, but they can't because they have no money, I want you to just explain to them that they don't need the money until they've made the decision to go on a vacation or to get the car. Once the decision is made, they'll figure out a way to get the money needed. They always do. A lot of times people try things once or twice and then throw in the towel and feel as if they are a failure, which then in turn causes low self-esteem and low confidence, which then causes ambivalence, and then the decisions going forward are not made confidently. Failing doesn't make anyone feel good, and failing does not make anyone a failure. However, quitting most certainly does. And quitting is a decision, and you would have to say when you make a decision to quit, you make a decision to fail. It's that simple.

Winning is a decision. Helen Keller was once asked if she thought there was anything worse than being blind. And I love this response. She replied, "The most pathetic person in the world is a person who has their sight but no vision." How great is that? You have sight but no vision. When a person has no vision of a better way of life, they automatically shut themselves in a prison and limit themselves to a life without hope. You have to have a vision. Imagination is one of your greatest assets. Everyone has a great imagination. You just have to practice, and we don't want a life without hope.

Stop worrying about where the resource is going to come from. I want you to picture this. Money is no object. I want you to make a firm decision to hold on to that vision. No matter what. Many people get a beautiful vision of how they would like to live, but because they can't see how they're going to make it happen or how they can get there, they let the vision go. Once you make the decision the resources will come into your life to help you reach that goal. They might not all come at once, they usually come a piece at a time, but when you see them come you'll know you're on your way. And by the way, if you knew how you're going to get what you were going after, that's not a vision, that's a plan.

Let me repeat that. If you knew how you're going to get it or to do it, you would have a plan, not a vision. There's no inspiration with a plan, but there is inspiration with a vision, and when you get the vision, freezeframe it with the decision and don't worry about how you're going to do it or where the resources are going to come from. Give your decision enthusiasm. This is really important to get excited about your decision and refuse to worry about what will happen. We make advanced bookings for flying and rental cars. Think of the problems you can eliminate by making many of the decisions well in advance.

Your life is important, and you have the potential to do anything you choose, and not only to do anything you choose, but the ability to do it well. But we have to make the decision, and when the time for decision arrives you must make your decision where you are with what you've got. William James said, "Compared to what we ought to be, we are making use of only a small part of our physical and mental resources."

The human individual lives far within his or her limits. He or she possesses powers of various sorts which he or she habitually fails to use. And that's kind of interesting, isn't it? Thomas Edison said, "If we all did the things we were capable of doing, we would literally astound ourselves by making a simple decision." The greatest minds of the past are available to you. Decide right now to start studying all these people that are great decision makers. You can literally learn how to turn your dreams into reality, and you have limitless resources of potential and ability waiting to be developed. So, let's start today.

I want you to have confidence in making decisions and be okay with whatever happens.

Now, this doesn't mean just run around and "Oh, Michael said make decisions. I'm going to decide to go to the casino and just spend my savings and try to make millions." That's not what I'm talking about. Be calculated. Do your homework, ask questions, but ultimately make the decision. Once you've made the decision you don't have to worry about all the other things you could be doing or other things that could go on, because the decision has been made. You also become very calm and in a peaceful state because you're working toward a decision you've made versus wondering, *What the heck should I do?* I'm peaceful, I'm calm, I'm moving in that direction. I am advancing. I got the blinders on like the horse so they can't see left or right. Just going forward. This is where I'm going, and you'll start getting excited because you'll see the resources coming into your life to help you on a daily basis.

I can't wait for you to start to see growth and a new spirit about yourself.

CONCLUSION

I want you to know I work on this material in this book every day. I am not a doctor and don't have all the answers, just a very motivated person who wants to help you. Just because I showed you this material doesn't mean I have it all figured out. I battle paradigms and read my goal card every day. I try my best to live by these laws so I can stay in a positive vibration. But you know what? I slip sometimes too. I self-doubt, get frustrated, second guess sometimes. However, I have learned through repetition to get out of those thoughts fast and get back to the way I want to feel, and you will too. This is not about being perfect, it is about self-development and living the life you have always wanted. And the learning and development will go on forever. The more you work on yourself, the faster you will recognize when you slide back to the old paradigms and can quickly bounce back. Remember, now you are aware of your feelings and are armed with the knowledge to bounce back and be amazing, which in turn will impact people around you in a positive way—and most importantly, yourself.

You've now learned what not many people know, and that's the secret to living the life you've always wanted and having the things you've always wanted. The life you've always wanted and the things you've always wanted are not just for certain people, they are for everyone. Your thinking mind is the most powerful thing in the entire planet, and what you've just learned is how to use it to your advantage.

You don't have to live the way you've been programmed to live. You don't have to feel the way you've been programmed to feel. The whole reason I wrote this book is I want you to understand you are amazing and have more potential than you'll ever use in your entire life. I also have a deep passion for helping people live the life they have always wanted and becoming what they have always wanted. I've learned how to do this, and I wanted to share these processes with you. You've learned how to change those nasty paradigms that are slowing you down from doing what you already know how to do. You also learned how to go after goals that really wake you up with fire and desire every morning, and you've learned there is a process to wealth and fulfillment, and it's not just the lucky birthright. Choose to live by these laws.

Becoming fulfilled and wealthy is about doing things a certain way, not doing a certain thing. My hope is you understand you have control of your life regardless of your environment, regardless of your heredity, and the cover of the book was designed around you and the genie. The genie will give you whatever you ask for. I want you to be the most amazing person you can be. I believe you have the ability to do anything in this world you want. You now have the steps to use your genie to your advantage and suggest to yourself amazing habits. The ultimate factor in all of this is making the decision. Make the decision today to live the life you've always wanted and become the person you've always wanted to be and put all those paradigms to rest that are slowing you down. I would go back and reread the book as many times as you can. You will get many things out of it the second, third, and fourth time. It is a book you can read for the rest of your life. I would love to know about your successes and when you accomplish your goals. I am pulling for you. You are amazing. The only thing I ask is when you see your amazing life start to improve you share this with someone who needs it. Pay it forward. Teach them what you have learned and be the inspiration they need. Use the Law of Increase to show them how special they are and point them on the path to living and feeling better. Be that glimmer of hope for someone who is in need. Be the encouragement they need no matter who they are. We all matter. We all need each other, and together nothing can stop us from living the life we have always wanted. If you are struggling in your life I personally want you to know I believe in you and wrote this book because of that belief in you. Maybe that is not logical, but we have already discussed logic. Logic, take a hike. I love how I live and feel every day, and I want you to know you can love yourself and your life too. And yes, I mean you. The world needs more love. The more we feel love in ourselves and work on ourselves, the more we can love and help others. Thank you for reading this book. Thank you for deciding to look at yourself in the mirror every day and start to believe you are amazing—because you are! Let's do this!

Made in the USA
Columbia, SC
26 June 2019